WAR PLANES

Stealth Bombers:
The B-2 Spirits

by Bill Sweetman

CAPSTONE
HIGH-INTEREST
BOOKS

an imprint of Capstone Press
Mankato, Minnesota

Capstone High-Interest Books are published by Capstone Press
151 Good Counsel Drive, P.O. Box 669, Mankato, Minnesota 56002
http://www.capstone-press.com

Library of Congress Cataloging-in-Publication Data
Sweetman, Bill.
    Stealth bombers: the B-2 Spirits/by Bill Sweetman.
    p. cm.—(War Planes)
    Includes bibliographical references and index.
    ISBN 0-7368-0791-8
    1. B-2 bomber—Juvenile literature. 2. Stealth aircraft—Juvenile literature.
[1. B-2 bomber. 2. Stealth aircraft.] I. Title. II. War Planes (Mankato, Minn.)
UG1242.B6 S9523 2001
623.7'463—dc21   00-010483

Summary: Discusses the B-2 Spirit, its uses, engines, weapons, and future in the
U.S. Air Force.

Editorial Credits
Matt Doeden, editor; Lois Wallentine, product planning editor; Timothy
    Halldin, cover designer and illustrator; Katy Kudela, photo researcher

Photo Credits
Official U.S. Air Force photo, 4, 6, 9, 10, 13, 18, 20, 22, 24, 27
Photri-Microstock, 28
Stocktrek, cover
Ted Carlson/Fotodynamics, 1, 16–17

**Special thanks to the U.S. Air Force Air Combat Command for their help in
preparing this book.**

1 2 3 4 5 6 06 05 04 03 02 01

Table of Contents

4

Chapter One

Learn About

- The B-2's mission
- Building the B-2
- The first B-2

The B-2 in Action

It is late at night. Two U.S. Air Force pilots climb into a strange-looking plane. They take off from Whiteman Air Force Base (AFB) in Missouri. The dark-gray plane is as big as a jetliner. But it has no body, no tail, and no engine pods. The plane is a B-2 Spirit.

The pilots fly the B-2 over the Atlantic Ocean toward Europe. There, enemy soldiers are invading a neighboring country. The U.S. military plans to attack an enemy air base in order to stop the invasion.

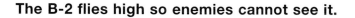

The B-2 flies high so enemies cannot see it.

The pilots fly the B-2 toward the enemy's capital city. But the city is well defended. The enemy has hundreds of surface-to-air missiles ready to launch at attacking aircraft. These missiles will destroy any enemy aircraft that radar instruments spot.

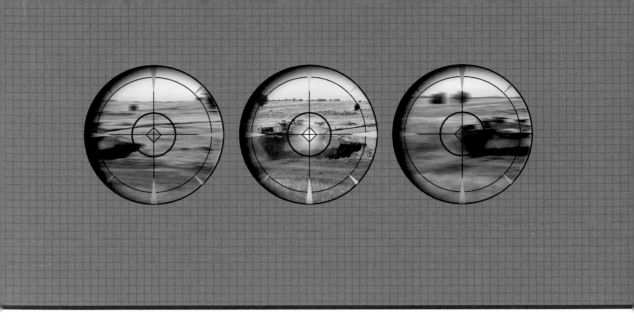

The B-2 pilots are safe from the enemy's missiles. The B-2 is a stealth aircraft. This means that radar cannot detect it easily. The enemy forces cannot launch missiles at the B-2 because they do not know it is there.

The B-2 pilots arrive at their target. An enemy air base stands almost 9 miles (14 kilometers) below them. The pilots open two huge doors on the plane's underside. The pilots release 16 bombs. The bombs fall to the ground and hit airplane hangars, fuel tanks, and airplanes. The explosions destroy the enemy air base. The mission is a success. The pilots turn around and return to Whiteman AFB.

About the B-2

The Northrop Grumman Corporation designed and built the B-2 Spirit. The U.S. military and Northrop Grumman worked together for almost 20 years to complete the B-2. It is one of the most advanced aircraft ever built. It also is the most expensive. Each B-2 costs about $1.3 billion to build.

The B-2 made its first test flight in July 1989. But that model was not ready for use. The U.S. Air Force did not receive completed B-2s until 1993. The first B-2 was called *The Spirit of Missouri*. The U.S. Air Force now has 21 B-2s. All 21 planes are based at Whiteman AFB in Missouri.

The Air Force first used the B-2 for military purposes in 1999. Pilots flew B-2s over Serbia in eastern Europe. For 11 weeks, B-2 pilots bombed Serbian targets. These

The first B-2 was called *The Spirit of Missouri*.

targets included air bases, bridges, railroads, and power plants. The bombing helped convince the Serbian government to pull its soldiers out of neighboring Kosovo.

Chapter Two

Learn About

- Stealth design
- Engine power
- Computer controls

Inside the B-2

The B-2 does not look like any other airplane. Most airplanes have a body, two wings, and a tail. The B-2 is a flying wing. The jet engines, cockpit, fuel, and bombs all are located inside the wing. The plane does not even have a tail. The front and rear edges of the wing are perfectly straight. The upper and lower surfaces are curved. The surfaces have no sharp edges or flat areas.

Stealth Design

The B-2 is so different because it is a stealth airplane. Enemies cannot easily spot the B-2. The B-2 weighs 150 tons (136 metric tons) and is 172 feet (52.1 meters) wide. But on radar, it appears no larger than a bird.

Radar instruments send radio signals through the air. Radio signals bounce off most solid objects. The radar detects the signals that bounce back from these objects. Radar devices use the signals that bounce back to determine an object's size and location.

Most planes are easy to see on radar. Their metal surfaces, flat body sides, and sharp corners strongly reflect the radio waves. Radar can detect most large bomber planes from as far as 300 miles (480 kilometers) away.

The B-2 is different. Its curved surface does not reflect radio waves strongly. The B-2 also is made of a different material than other planes. Most planes are made of aluminum. Radar waves bounce easily off this metal. The B-2 is made of carbon fiber. This material is made of strong, thin fibers held together by plastic. Carbon fiber is stronger and more lightweight

21070

than most metals. It does not reflect radar waves as strongly as metals do.

Designers made special plastic material for the edges of the B-2's wing. Radar waves do not bounce off the plastic. Designers also knew that small gaps in the B-2's surface could be detected by radar. Every door and cover on the plane must fit perfectly.

Engines

The B-2 has four General Electric F-118 jet engines. The engines produce thrust. This force pushes the airplane through the air. Each engine creates about 17,300 pounds (7,850 kilograms) of thrust.

Most jet engines are on the outside of the plane. Radar easily detects the engines. The B-2's designers placed the plane's engines in the thickest part of the wing. They curved the engines' inlets and outlets. Air enters and exits the jet engines through these openings. The curving helps hide the engines from radar.

Jet engines sometimes create contrails during flight. These white, cloudy trails are formed by water that comes out of the jet engines' outlets. Contrails make a B-2 visible to enemies. But contrails only are visible at certain heights. The B-2 has a laser radar that warns the pilot if the plane's contrail is visible. The pilot then can make the contrail disappear by flying higher or lower.

Gauges and Controls

Pilots use gauges to keep track of their position. Some gauges tell pilots their planes' speed, altitude, and direction. Other gauges track enemy targets.

B-2 Specifications

Function:	Heavy bomber
Manufacturer:	Northrop Grumman Corporation
Date Deployed:	1993
Length:	69 feet (20.9 meters)
Wingspan:	172 feet (52.1 meters)
Engines:	Four General Electric F-118-GE-100 engines
Thrust:	17,300 pounds (7,850 kilograms) per engine
	69,200 pounds (31,400 kilograms) total
Speed:	Classified
Ceiling:	50,000 feet (15,152 meters)
Range:	6,000 miles (9,655 kilometers)

Most of the B-2's systems are controlled by computers. For example, the B-2 does not have a tail. The lack of a tail makes the plane difficult to control. Small movements of the wing flaps can make the plane spin out of control. But computers constantly adjust the flaps to keep the B-2 stable. The computers may adjust the wing flaps as many as 40 times per second.

engine intake

wing flap

landing gear

The B-2 Spirit

cockpit

nose

landing gear

Chapter Three

Learn About

- Smart bombs
- Mission planning
- Safety measures

Weapons and Tactics

The B-2 carries bombs and missiles. The total weight of these bombs and missiles is called the payload. The B-2 can carry a payload of as much as 40,000 pounds (18,000 kilograms).

The B-2 drops most of its weapons through its two bomb bays. These openings are on the bottom of the airplane. They are located on the middle part of the wing. The B-2's main weapons are smart bombs and air-to-ground missiles. These weapons are used to attack ground targets such as enemy bases and roads.

Smart bombs are the B-2's main weapon.

Bombs and Missiles

Smart bombs are the B-2's main weapon. Computers control these guided weapons. The B-2's main bomb is the Joint Direct Attack Munition (JDAM). The JDAM has a Global Positioning System (GPS) receiver in its tail. Satellites orbiting Earth send signals to this device. The signals guide the JDAM to an exact location. Some B-2s carry the Joint Stand-Off

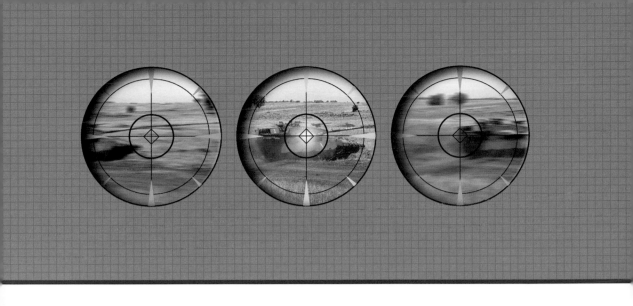

Weapon (JSOW). This smart bomb is another version of the JDAM.

The Lockheed Martin AGM-158 is one of the U.S. Air Force's newest weapons. This missile is called the Joint Air-to-Surface Standoff Missile (JASSM). The JASSM is like a miniature stealth airplane. It has wings and a small jet engine. It can fly more than 200 miles (320 kilometers) after launch. The JASSM is guided by heat-seeking equipment in its nose.

The EGBU-28 is another new B-2 weapon. This long, narrow bomb weighs 4,700 pounds (2,130 kilograms). The EGBU-28 is useful when enemies have hidden weapons deep underground. It can destroy targets that are as much as 100 feet (30 meters) underground.

The B-2 can refuel while in the air.

Staying Safe

A B-2 pilot's main goal is to remain undetected. Most B-2 missions take place at night. The Air Force carefully plans B-2 missions so pilots do not fly over an enemy during daylight.

Before a mission, the military gathers information about the enemy. It uses spy planes such as the U-2 to make maps of an enemy's territory. Military experts look at these maps. They search for possible targets. They also search for enemy radar. Some powerful radar stations can detect B-2s that are almost directly overhead. B-2 pilots must fly around these stations.

The B-2 is designed to fly long missions. Its range is more than 6,000 miles (9,655 kilometers). It can fly this distance without refueling. The B-2 also can refuel from a tanker aircraft in the air. Pilots must be able to withstand long missions lasting nearly a day. Two pilots usually fly each B-2. The pilots may take turns taking short naps during a mission.

B-2 pilots often must use their own judgment on missions. They do not use radios when they are near an enemy. The radio signals could give away their position. Pilots cannot contact their commanders once they are near enemy territory.

Chapter Four

Learn About

- The B-2's future
- Joint lines
- New equipment

The Future

The B-2 is among the U.S. Air Force's most important aircraft. But the U.S. military does not plan to buy any more B-2s. The bombers cost too much. The military will buy smaller, less expensive bombers instead. It also will keep its current B-2s in service for many years to come.

Filling the Gaps

B-2 ground crews spend a great deal of time working on the planes. Ground crews must remove pieces of the B-2's outer surface when they check or fix parts underneath. Ground crews must then carefully fit the skin back into place. This leaves small gaps called joint lines. Ground crews must fill the joint lines with a special paste. This paste takes several hours to dry properly.

Engineers and chemists are developing new materials to fill in joint lines. These materials will seal joint lines better. They also will dry more quickly.

Ground crews also have started using tools to check joint lines. They use a radar device set on a forklift to check the planes. The radar detects any gaps caused by joint lines.

Ground crews repair B-2s on the ground.

The Air Force plans to use the B-2 until at least 2020.

New Equipment

The U.S. Air Force is changing the computers inside B-2s. The B-2's original computers were designed in the 1980s. Computers are much faster and more powerful today.

The Air Force also plans to equip the B-2 with a satellite radio link. This communication device will allow pilots to receive large amounts of information during flight. Pilots will be able to see updated photos of a target taken hours before an attack.

The U.S. military hopes that these improvements will keep future B-2 pilots safe. The Air Force plans to use the B-2 bomber until at least 2020. In future conflicts, it will be among the first U.S. aircraft to fly into action.

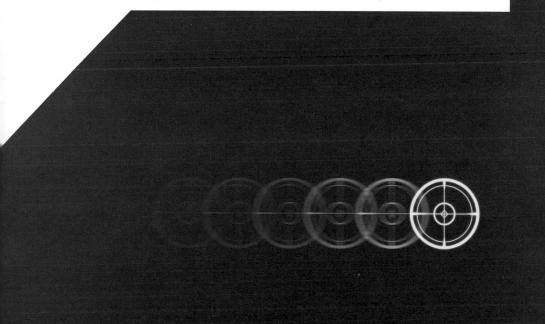

Words to Know

aluminum (uh-LOO-mi-nuhm)—a lightweight, silver-colored metal; most airplanes are made of aluminum.

carbon fiber (KAR-buhn FYE-bur)—a material made of strong, thin fibers held together by plastic; the outside parts of B-2s are made of carbon fiber.

contrail (KON-trayl)—a white, cloudy trail of water that comes out of a jet engine

gauge (GAYJ)—an instrument that measures a property such as speed or direction

mission (MISH-uhn)—a military task

payload (PAY-lohd)—the total weight of the bombs and missiles that a B-2 carries

radar (RAY-dar)—equipment that uses radio waves to locate and guide objects

thrust (THRUHST)—the force created by a jet engine; thrust pushes an airplane forward.

To Learn More

Chant, Christopher. *Fighters and Bombers.* The World's Greatest Aircraft. Philadelphia: Chelsea House Publishers, 1999.

Green, Michael. *The United States Air Force.* Serving Your Country. Mankato, Minn.: Capstone High-Interest Books, 1998.

Maynard, Christopher. *Aircraft.* The Need for Speed. Minneapolis: Lerner Publications, 1999.

Useful Addresses

Air Combat Command
Office of Public Affairs
115 Thompson Street, Suite 211
Langley AFB, VA 23665

Air Force History Support Office
Reference and Analysis Division
200 McChord Street, Box 94
Bolling AFB, DC 20332-1111

Internet Sites

Air Force Link
http://www.af.mil

FAS Nuclear Forces Guide—B-2 Spirit
http://www.fas.org/nuke/guide/usa/bomber/
    b-2.htm

Smithsonian National Air and Space Museum
http://www.nasm.edu

Index